greatest **hits** so far...✪

madonna ✪

IMP

International MUSIC Publications

International Music Publications Limited
Griffin House 161 Hammersmith Road London W6 8BS England

Production: Miranda Steel
Cover design: Glide Design

Published 1999

Beautiful Stranger

Words and Music by
MADONNA CICCONE and WILLIAM ORBIT

1. Have-n't we met?____

You're some kind of beau-ti-ful strang-er.

You could be good_

strang - er.____ Da da da da da da da da da da da da da.____

Beau - ti - ful strang - er.____

Repeat ad lib. and fade

Crazy For You

Words and Music by
JOHN BETTIS and JON LIND

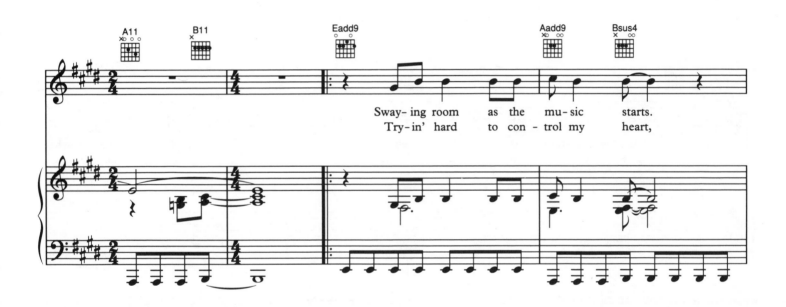

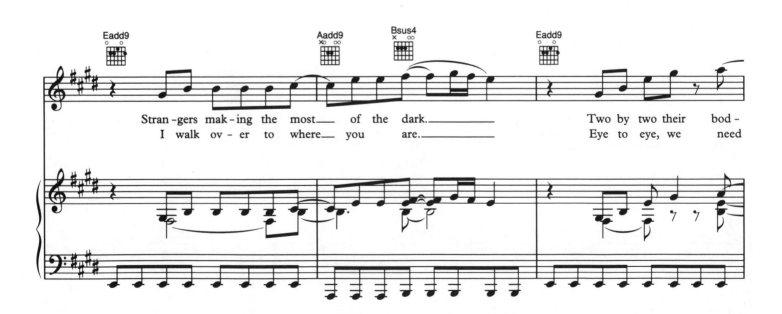

Sway- ing room as the mu- sic starts.
Try- in' hard to con- trol my heart,

Stran -gers mak- ing the most of the dark.
I walk ov- er to where you are.

Two by two their bod-
Eye to eye, we need

Holiday

Words and Music by
LISA STEVENS and **CURTIS HUDSON**

Like A Virgin

Words and Music by
TOM KELLY and BILLY STEINBERG

Like A Prayer

Words and Music by
MADONNA CICCONE and PATRICK LEONARD

Frozen

Words and Music by
MADONNA CICCONE and PATRICK LEONARD

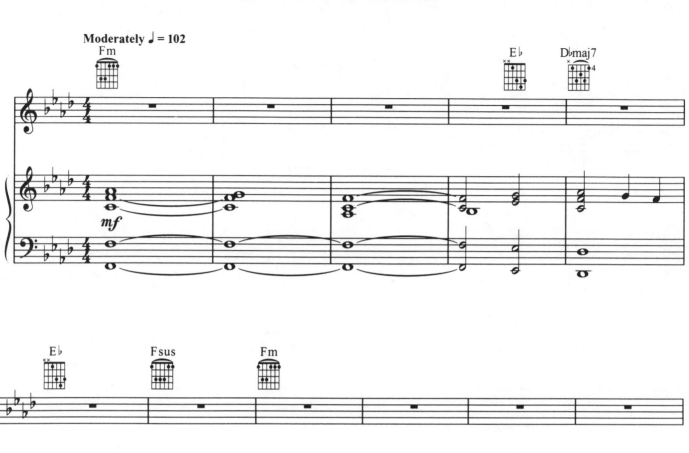

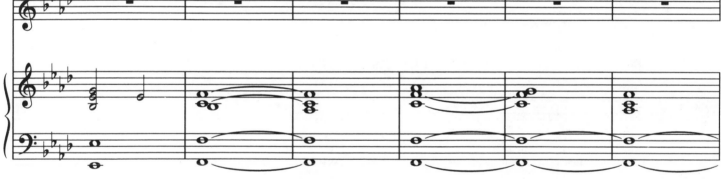

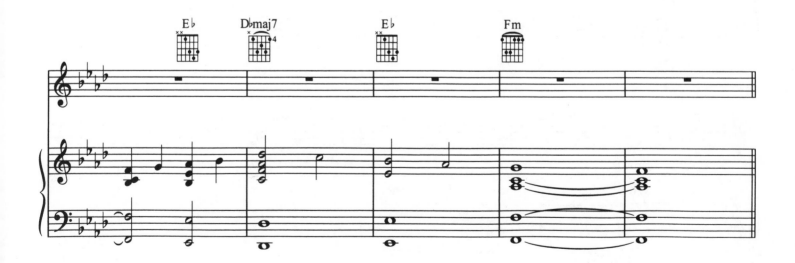

Papa Don't Preach

Words and Music by BRIAN ELLIOT
Additional lyrics by MADONNA CICCONE

Ray Of Light

Words and Music by
MADONNA CICCONE, WILLIAM ORBIT, CLIVE MULDOON, DAVE CURTIS and CHRISTINE LEACH

And I feel,___ like I just___ got home,_ and I feel._

To Coda ⊕

1.

2.

44

Material Girl

Words and Music by
PETER BROWN and ROBERT RANS

This Used To Be My Playground

Words and Music by
MADONNA CICCONE and SHEP PETTIBONE

Who's That Girl?

Words and Music by
MADONNA CICCONE and PATRICK LEONARD

60